odorou

H www.heinemann.co.uk
Visit our website to find out more information about **Heinemann Library** books.

To order:
☎ Phone 44 (0) 1865 888066
🗎 Send a fax to 44 (0) 1865 314091
💻 Visit the Heinemann Bookshop at www.heinemann.co.uk to browse our catalogue and order online.

First published in Great Britain by Heinemann Library, Halley Court, Jordan Hill, Oxford OX2 8EJ, a division of Reed Educational and Professional Publishing Ltd. Heinemann is a registered trademark of Reed Educational & Professional Publishing Limited.

OXFORD MELBOURNE AUCKLAND JOHANNESBURG BLANTYRE
GABORONE IBADAN PORTSMOUTH NH (USA) CHICAGO

© Reed Educational and Professional Publishing Ltd 2000
The moral right of the proprietor has been asserted.

Designed by Ron Kamen
Illustrations by Dewi Morris/Robert Sydenham
Originated by Ambassador Litho Ltd.
Printed by South China Printing in Hong Kong / China

ISBN 0431 00128 6 (hardback)   ISBN 0431 00147 2 (paperback)
04 03 02 01 00   04 03 02 01
10 9 8 7 6 5 4 3 2 1   10 9 8 7 6 5 4 3 2 1

British Library Cataloguing in Publication Data
Theodorou, Rod
    Black rhino - (Animals in danger)
    1.Black rhinoceros - Juvenile literature 2.Endangered species - Juvenile literature
    I.Title
    599.6'68

Acknowledgements
The Publishers would like to thank the following for permission to reproduce photographs:
Ardea London: pg.13, RF Porter pg.23; Corbis: pg.11; *FLPA*: Gerard Lacz pg.4, David Hosking pg.5, pg.22, W Wisniewski pg.6, Eichhorn Zingel pg.8, Frants Hartmann pg.19, pg.21; *Mike Johnson*: pg.4; *NHPA*: Martin Harvey pg.18, Daryl Balfour pg.25; *Oxford Scientific Films*: pg.16, Daniel J Cox pg.4, Tom Leach pg.7, pg.9, Stan Osolonski pg.12, Konrad Wothe pg.14, Steve Turner pg.15, pg.24, David Cayless pg.20; *Still Pictures*: M & C Denis-Huot pg.17, Michel Gunther pg.26, Roland Seitre pg.27

Cover photograph reproduced with permission of Bruce Coleman.

Our thanks to Henning Dräger of WWF-UK for his comments in the preparation of this book.

Every effort has been made to contact copyright holders of any material reproduced in this book. Any omissions will be rectified in subsequent printings if notice is given to the Publisher.

Contents

Any words appearing in the text in bold, **like this**, are explained in the Glossary.

Animals in danger

blue whale

Bengal tiger

Florida manatee

All over the world, more than 10,000 animal **species** are in danger. Some are in danger because their home is being **destroyed.** Many are in danger because people hunt them.

This book is about black rhinos and why they are in danger. Unless people learn to protect them, black rhinos will become **extinct**. We will only be able to find out about them from books like this.

What is a rhino?

Rhinos are huge **mammals**. There are five different **species** of rhino. The two largest species are the black rhino and the white rhino. This picture shows a white rhino.

Black and white rhinos are both grey in colour.
White rhinos have wide, square lips. Black rhinos
have a pointed, hooked lip like a parrot's beak.
This picture shows a black rhino.

What does a rhino look like?

Rhinos have huge bodies. They have four short thick legs with three stumpy toes on each. Their skin is grey and very thick, like armour. They are heavy but they can move very quickly.

Some rhinos have only one horn, but the black rhino has two horns. The horns are very hard and are used to protect the rhino from **predators**. A black rhino's horn can grow over 1 metre long!

Where do rhinos live?

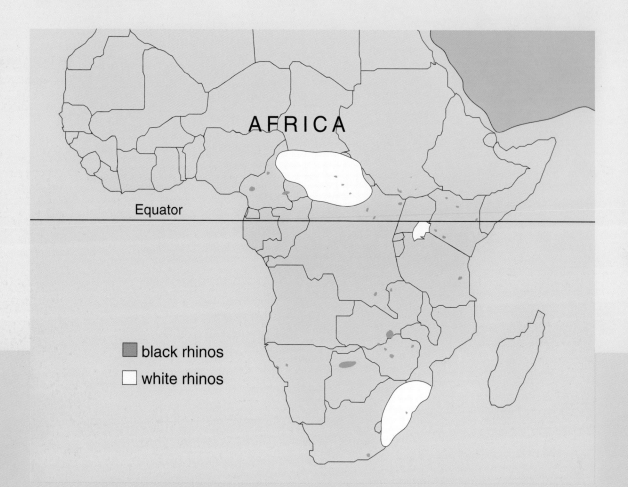

AFRICA

Equator

■ black rhinos
□ white rhinos

Black and white rhinos both live in Africa. White rhinos like open **savannah** where they can munch away on grass. Black rhinos like to live on the edge of forests amongst bushes and trees.

10

The Indian, Javan and Sumatran rhinos live in Asia. The Javan and Sumatran rhinos live deep inside thick rainforests where they can find leaves and fruit to eat. The Indian rhino likes wallowing in cool, muddy swamps and marshes.

What do black rhinos eat?

Rhinos only eat plants and fruits. Black rhinos use their hooked lip to pluck off leaves or pull down small trees to eat the fruit.

Black rhinos feed in the morning and late into the evening. They do not like the very hot sun. They try to find a shady place to rest during the heat of the day.

Black rhino babies

Black rhinos do not live in family groups. They like to live alone and only come together to **mate**. When they have mated the **male** leaves. He does not help to look after the baby.

14

The **female** usually only has one baby. The baby is called a calf. The calf can stand up about an hour after it is born. It feeds on its mother's milk.

Looking after the calf

The calf only has a small bump for a horn, but it grows quickly. It will live with its mother for two or three years, and then live on its own.

Hyenas and lions sometimes attack baby black rhinos. The mother will charge at any **predator** that comes near her calf. Black rhinos can be very fierce if they feel they are in danger.

Unusual rhino facts

Black rhinos cannot see very well, but they have a very good sense of smell. They only have hair at the ends of their tails and on their eyelids and the tips of their ears.

These white rhinos live in **herds** and are not very dangerous. Black rhinos live alone and sometimes may charge people who come too close.

How many black rhinos are there?

One hundred years ago there were about one million black rhinos in Africa. Now there are fewer than 1900 of them in the wild, even though they are **protected** by **law**.

Black rhinos are being killed faster than any other large animal on Earth. Over 73,000 have been killed in the last 30 years!

Why is the black rhino in danger?

People shoot black rhinos and then cut off their horns to sell them. Many horns go to China to be **ground** down and sold as medicine.

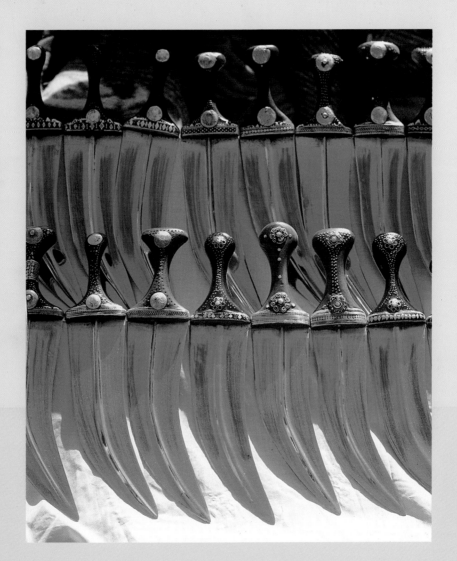

Many horns are sold to a country called Yemen.
They are made into the handles of **daggers,** like
the ones in this picture, for Yemeni men.

How is the black rhino being helped?

Many leaders in China and Yemen are trying to stop people selling rhino horn. All African and Asian countries have made rhino hunting against the **law**. This black rhino has his own guard!

Conservation groups like the World Wide Fund for Nature (WWF) are also working to stop **poaching** and save the rhino. These two young black rhinos are being looked after because their mothers were killed by poachers.

25

How is the black rhino being helped?

In some countries black rhinos are caught and their horns are cut off and burned. This does not hurt the rhino and it stops hunters **poaching** them until the horns grow back.

Many African countries have places where the rhinos are **protected** by fences and guards. This is the best way to save the black rhino.

Rhino factfile

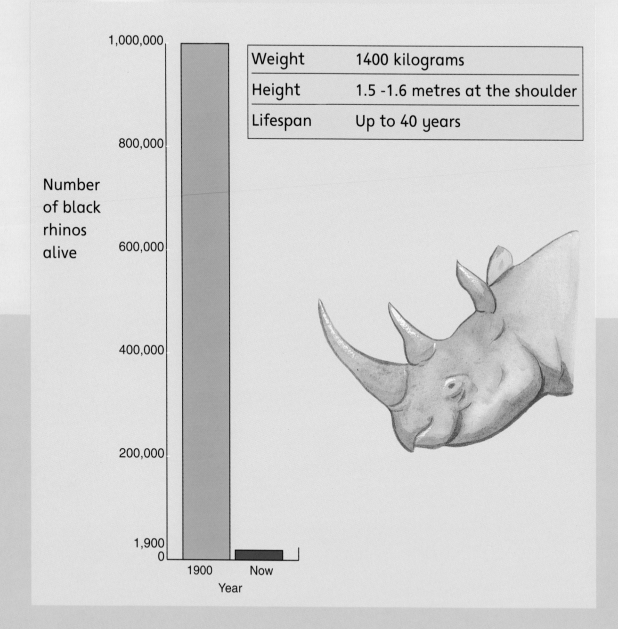

Weight	1400 kilograms
Height	1.5 -1.6 metres at the shoulder
Lifespan	Up to 40 years

Number of black rhinos alive

1,000,000
800,000
600,000
400,000
200,000
1,900
0

1900   Now

Year

World danger table

	Number that may have been alive 100 years ago	Number that may be alive today
Giant panda	65,000	650
Bengal tiger	100,000	4500
Blue whale	335,000	4000
Mountain gorilla	85,000	500
Florida manatee	75,000	1400

There are thousands of other animals in the world that are in danger of becoming **extinct**. This table shows some of these animals.

Can you find out more about them?

Further reading, addresses and websites

Books

Rhinoceroses, Endangered! series, Amanda Harman, Benchmark Books, Marshall Cavendish, 1997

Rhino, Caroline Arnold, Morrow Junior Books, 1995

Rhinos, Wildlife at Risk series, Malcolm Penny, Wayland, 1991

The African Rhino, Animals in Danger series, William R. Sanford and Carl R. Green, Heinemann, 1990

Vanishing Species, Green Issues series, Miles Barton, Franklin Watts, 1997

Organizations

Friends of the Earth: UK - 26-28 Underwood Street, London, N1 7JQ ☎ (020) 7490 1555
Australia - 312 Smith Street, Collingwood, Vic 3065 ☎ 03 9419 8700

Greenpeace: UK - Canonbury Villas, London, N1 2PN ☎ (020) 7865 8100
Australia - Level 4, 39 Liverpool Street, Sydney, NSW 2000 ☎ 02 9261 4666

WWF: UK - Panda House, Weyside Park, Catteshall Lane, Godalming, Surrey GU7 1XR ☎ (01483) 426 444
Australia - Level 5, 725 George Street, Sydney, NSW 2000 ☎ 02 9281 5515

Useful Websites

www.bbc.co.uk/nature/
The BBC's animals site. Go to Really Wild for information on all sorts of animals, including fun activities, the latest news, and links to programmes.

www.defenders.org
A conservation group dedicated to protecting animals and plants. Go to Kids Planet on their site.

www.rhinos-irf.org
The International Rhino Foundation's site, dedicated to the conservation of the rhino.

www.sandiegozoo.org
The world-famous American San Diego Zoo's site. Go to the Pick an Animal section for games and factsheets.

www.wwf.org
The World Wildlife Fund For Nature (WWF) is the world's largest independent conservation organization. The WWF conserves wildlife and the natural environment for present and future generations.

Glossary

conservation	looking after something, especially if it is in danger
dagger	a sharp, pointed knife with a handle
destroyed	spoilt, broken or torn apart so it can't be used
extinct	a species that has completely died out and can never live again
female	the opposite of a male, such as a girl or woman
ground	crushed into powder
herd	a group of the same animals living together
law	a rule or something you have to do
male	the opposite of a female, such as a boy or a man
mammals	warm-blooded animals, like humans, that feed their young on their mother's milk
mate	when a male animal and a female animal come together to make baby animals
poachers/poaching	poachers are hunters who make money from hunting (poaching) animals to sell parts of their bodies like teeth, bones and fur
predator	animal that hunts and kills other animals
protected	looked after, sometimes by law
savannah	large areas of grassland with few trees
species	a group of living things that are very similar

Index